True Faith

True Faith

Reflections on Paul's Letter to Titus

PAUL JEON

WIPF *&* STOCK · Eugene, Oregon

TRUE FAITH
Reflections on Paul's Letter to Titus

Wipf & Stock
An Imprint of Wipf and Stock Publishers
199 W. 8th Ave., Suite 3
Eugene, OR 97401

www.wipfandstock.com

ISBN 13: 978-1-62032-023-5

Manufactured in the U.S.A.

This work is dedicated to my wife who continues to model what it means to live according to the hope of eternal life.

Contents

Foreword

HAVING SERVED a number of years alongside Dr. Jeon in pastoral ministry, I have seen firsthand the rare marriage of scholarship and shepherding. To be sure, there is a necessary place for biblical scholarship in the academy, however removed from ecclesiastical affairs. Likewise, not every pastor is called to academic pursuits on a professional level. But every so often, God sees fit to gift certain of His servants with scholarly abilities and accomplishments that find their truest home not in the ivory tower, but in the local church. For those under his pastoral care, Dr. Jeon's devotion to understanding and teaching the Word of God has always coincided with his love for the people of God.

True Faith is an example of this beautiful coincidence. The following work is neither purely academic nor purely "applicational" in its treatment of the apostle Paul's letter to Titus. Rather, it is the fruit of a scholar-shepherd's commitment to engage God's Word on the deepest level for the specific purpose of building up its intended audience, the local church. After all, such a commitment is true to the letter itself. As you will discover throughout, true faith in Jesus Christ is not simply a matter of correct theology per se, but that theology must work itself out in how Christians engage one another and the world around them. Or as the apostle puts it in 1:1, he writes "for the sake of the faith of God's elect and their knowledge of the truth, *which accords with godliness.*"

I have had the privilege of working through an early version of this commentary in the context of our local church, where God has used it to bring the message of Titus home to many. My prayer is that He would use this finished version similarly for you, the reader. May your reflections on the text, your own church community, and the culture in which He has placed you result in a life of true faith expressed in good works, as you await "our blessed hope, the appearing of the glory of our great God and Savior Jesus Christ." (2:13)

—Jimmy Choi
Worship Director, NewCity Church
November 3, 2011

Preface

IBEGAN writing my dissertation on Paul's letter to Titus in the fall of 2010 and completed it the following year. (This was truly by the grace of God given that during this time I was serving as a pastor. Had it not been for the support of my family and friends—especially my wife—I am confident that I would have left my doctorate program with an ABD.) I then spent the next six months preparing the dissertation for publication, which will soon be published by Wipf & Stock under the title *Titus: Exhort and Reprove to Commendable Works according to the Hope of Eternal Life*.

This is to say that I've spent a good deal of time thinking through this letter. My dissertation applied a new outline for the entire letter based on the literary device commonly referred to as a chiasm (most simply explained as an A-B-C-B'-A' structure for a collection of words and/or statements). The dissertation is inaccessible to those outside of academia and without a strong background in biblical Greek. The letter of Titus, however, has much to offer and yet remains one of the more neglected letters in the New Testament. For this reason, I wanted to write a brief introductory work on Titus, reflecting some of my gleanings from two years of pondering over the letter. Most commentaries on Titus include the letter under the broader discussion of the Pastoral Letters, which includes 1 and 2 Timothy. I believe, however, that a careful study of the letter should begin by treating the letter on its own, without undue reliance on what Saint Paul wrote in 1 and 2 Timothy.

The main purpose of this book is to reflect on the nature of true faith from the perspective of Paul's letter to Titus. My hope is that the reader will not only be stirred to take up a more detailed exposition of the entire letter but will continue to think through the meaning and implications of true faith. We live in an age where it has become too easy for one to claim to be a believer. Perhaps this is partially because we are afraid of being categorized as bigoted exclusivists. Nevertheless, the Bible, as we see in this letter, calls us to think through more circumspectly what it means to really believe in God.

Following my first book *Introducing Romans*, this brief study highlights the major themes of the letter by using Titus itself as an acronym (see Chapter One). In addition, this book presents the themes by following the flow of the letter (1:1-3:15) with the hope that the reader will gain both an appreciation of some of the more important themes of the letter and a sense of its rhetorical strategy.

I take full responsibility for the shortcomings of this work. Nevertheless, I wish to express my gratitude to several groups of individuals. First, I want to thank my parents whose contributions to all my works are ineffable. I also want to thank my brother, Abraham Jeon, and sister, Mary Lee, whose continual personal and financial support have made my writing projects possible. Second, I thank Ms. Su Jin Kim who continues to serve as careful, humble, and insightful editor. Third, I thank NewCity, my church with whom I am able to learn and apply the truths contained in this letter. A special thanks to Jimmy, Brian, James, Ji, and Paul.

Finally, I am most grateful to my wife, my persevering friend who has taught me what it means to do all things without complaining.

—Paul S. Jeon
August 3, 2011

1

Introduction

BRIEF BACKGROUND COMMENTS TO TITUS

SAINT PAUL wrote this letter to Titus and the believers[1] in Crete to help establish order among the churches and to remind them to call one another to live commendably in view of their hope of eternal life. Trouble was brewing among the churches with the increasing influence of rebellious and deceitful individuals who were upsetting the faith of many by teaching what they should not for greedy gain (1:101–1).[2] From the outset, therefore, Paul highlights both his authority as a slave of God and apostle of Christ Jesus and his unique status in God's plan of salvation as one who

---

1. That this letter was not intended solely for Titus is seen in the plural use of "you" in the closing blessing, "Grace be with you *all*" (3:15).

2. All translations are mine unless indicated otherwise. I have tried to keep my translations as literal as possible, and so at times the reader may find them somewhat awkward. Literal translations, however, are sometimes helpful for observing the rhetorical strategy of the assumed author (Saint Paul).

was entrusted with the very word of God (1:3). Moreover, for this reason the letter begins with a reiteration to Titus, Paul's reliable colleague, to appoint elders in every town who will alongside Titus deal with the troublemakers (1:5).

While we do not have a great deal of information on Titus, Paul's other letters indicate he was one of the apostle's most trustworthy partners for gospel ministry. Galatians 2:3 suggests that Titus joined the apostle early on in Paul's ministry. In 2 Corinthians (see 2:13; 7:6–16; 8:16–24) Titus seems to play the role of an intervention-specialist, addressing difficult issues among believers in Corinth and overseeing the special collection for the saints in need. In the letter addressed to him, Titus continues this role of carrying out Paul's directives under precarious and difficult circumstances.

The quote by the Cretan prophet in 1:12 aptly summarizes the notoriety of Crete: "Cretans are always liars, evil beasts, and lazy gluttons." Crete was an island located south of Greece and west of Asia Minor. It was an ideal location for sea trade and piracy and quickly became a place of debauchery, violence, gluttony, and duplicity. The Cretans were perhaps best known for their high claim of being the guardians of Zeus's birthplace and tomb on Mount Ida. Thus, consistent with the infamy of Zeus himself, the Cretans earned the reputation of being proud liars who viewed lying as an admirable quality. This historical context helps explain Paul's careful description of God as the one "who cannot lie" (1:2) and his repeated emphasis on living consistently with one's embrace of the truth (1:1).

KEY THEMES

Paul's letter to Titus can be summarized under five themes, which are covered by the acronym "TITUS": (1) *T*rue Faith (1:1–4); (2) *I*rreproachable Leaders (1:5–16); (3) *T*heocentric Household (2:1–15); (4) *U*pright Citizens (3:1–8a); and (5) *S*teadfast Devotion to Good Works (3:8b–15). The chapters that follow will go into more detail on each theme. Here I want to discuss how these five themes are interconnected under the broader theme of "Exhorting and Reproving One Another to Good Works according to the Hope of Eternal Life."

Paul never deviates in this letter from his gospel, which declares that a person is not saved by works but through faith in Jesus Christ. That is, salvation comes to those who do not trust in their own good works but believe that Jesus lived the life that they should have lived, died the death that they should have died, so that by his life, death, and resurrection they would share in the hope of eternal life. That Paul maintains this gospel message is reflected in his description of the letter's recipients as "God's elect" (those who have been chosen by God, 1:1) who have been redeemed through Christ's self-sacrifice (2:14) not according to their righteous works but according to God's mercy (3:5).

Nevertheless, there is a strong emphasis in this letter on living a life characterized by commendable works. Paul's basic contention is that while a person is not saved by his good works, good works demonstrate that a person is truly saved. In other words, while good works do not result in salvation, they evidence the reality of one's salvation. Specifically, in this letter Paul asserts that those who await the hope of eternal life (1:2; 2:13; 3:7) ought to exhibit life-styles characterized by the renunciation of wickedness and the pursuit of godliness, expressed namely in a steadfast devotion to good works both inside and outside of the church. Such is the nature of true faith, which couples an embrace of the truth with the pursuit of righteousness.

Such a pursuit by those within a theocentric household, i.e., the community of faith united by its common hope, depends directly on mutual exhortation and reproof. Specifically, it depends on the exhortation and reproof of irreproachable leaders—in contrast to false teachers—who live commendably, especially within their own homes, and who hold fast to the word of truth that was first given through the apostle (1:5–9). These leaders model the kind of lifestyle and commitment to speaking truth that should be true for all who belong to the household of God.

APPROACH OF THE STUDY

Each theme in Titus will be explored from three angles: (1) Reflections on the Bible, (2) Reflections on Church, and (3) Reflections on Culture.

Reflections on the Bible

Chapters Two to Six each begins with a basic outline of the selected Bible passage. The outline provides an overview of what the passage is about. The outline is followed by some comments that highlight the structure of the passage and key terms. This effort to understand what Paul originally meant is necessary to have a meaningful discussion on how to apply Paul's teachings today. To enhance your understanding of Paul's intent/teaching/original meaning, I recommend reviewing the selected Bible passage before and after reading through my comments, and writing notes and questions throughout the entire process.

Reflections on Church

Although Titus is often interpreted as a letter written from one individual to another, it was written—as noted above—for the community of faith in Crete and contains topics (e.g., leadership, mutual exhortation and reproof) that are easily applicable to churches today. We will, therefore, spend some time reflecting on how Paul's teaching in Titus instructs us on how we are to think about and live in community.

Reflections on Culture

Titus, like 1 Timothy, is often treated like a manual for churches. What is missed, however, is its outward—missiological—thrust. Cretan believers are to be different from their surrounding Cretan culture not merely for the sake of being different but to bring honor to the word of God. For instance, the Christian slaves are reminded to be trustworthy in all things so that their masters, who (presumably) were unbelievers, "might adorn the doctrine of God our Savior" (2:10).[3] Titus, then, is a letter that was intended to instruct Christians on the kind of lifestyle that would

3. In passing, we should note that "slavery" meant something very different from the way it is used and understood today. Without going into detail, I will simply note that the Bible does *not* condone "modern" slavery. In fact, slave-traders are among those listed among the "ungodly and sinful" in 1 Timothy 1:8–10.

win the respect of their surrounding community. We will, therefore, conclude each chapter with some brief reflections on how Paul's teaching relates to our present calling to be the light of this world.

AN OUTLINE OF TITUS

2

True Faith

REFLECTIONS ON TITUS 1:1–4

Titus 1:1–4 is a single sentence in the Greek. The opening passage, however, is easier to understand if we break it down into three sub-units:

1:1   Paul, Slave of God, Apostle of Christ Jesus

1:2–3   The Hope of Eternal Life from the Unlying God

1:4   Titus, True Child according to the Faith

In the opening verse of the letter, Paul exhibits both tremendous confidence and humility: "Paul, slave of God, apostle of Jesus Christ" (1:1a). On the one hand, to be a slave and apostle (one who is sent to represent another) is to adopt a submissive and loyal posture to one's master and sender. On the other hand, to be a slave of *God* and apostle of *Jesus Christ* is to be one with authority. For this reason, Paul expects the recipients of this letter to submit to him out of reverence for God and Jesus Christ, for to acknowledge

Paul is to acknowledge the one he serves and the one who has sent him to convey a message to the Cretan believers.

Paul specifies that he has been sent specifically for the "faith of God's elect," i.e., to further their belief in God. The meaning of "faith of God's elect" is clarified by the phrase "embrace of the truth that accords with godliness" (1:1b). Most translations read something akin to "knowledge of the truth that results in godliness." These translations are inadequate because Paul does not have in view merely a knowledge of the truth (e.g., "I know that Jesus is the Son of God") but, rather, an embrace—a full recognition and acceptance—of the truth (e.g., "I believe wholeheartedly that Jesus is the Son of God"). Such an embrace must be accompanied by godliness, which means respectable deeds out of reverence for God. From the outset, then, Paul makes clear that recognition of the truth must be accompanied by good deeds. Such faith is true faith.

In the next sub-unit Paul states that the basis of his own faithfulness—the reason he endures hardship as a slave of God and apostle of Jesus Christ—is "the hope of eternal life." Hope, as we know from Paul's other letters, does not refer to something that we wish for but may or may not happen.[1] Rather, the hope of eternal life—the prospect of participating in God's eternal mode of existence—was promised by the unlying God—the God who cannot lie simply because it is counter to His being. Moreover, such a promise is sure for God's elect because it was given "before time began." Therefore, the hope is a sure hope because it

1. For a more detailed discussion of Christian hope, see Paul Jeon, *Introducing Romans* (Eugene, OR: Wipf&Stock, 2011), 35–41.

does not depend on whether one has been naughty or nice, but on God's trustworthy nature.

Verse 3 takes a sudden turn. There is a shift in focus from the hope of eternal life to the word of God that has been entrusted to the apostle and revealed in his proclamation. This shift is intentional, bringing to prominence the word of God, which the apostle will return to repeatedly in this letter. Paul's point is that although the promise of eternal life was made before eternal times, it has now been revealed in history through his gospel proclamation. Lest his audience perceive an element of pride, Paul concludes this verse by reiterating his position as "one who has been entrusted according to the command of God our Savior." A full embrace of the truth, then, can be nothing other than a full embrace of Paul's proclamation, given it is the word of God.

This first unit concludes with Paul wishing grace and peace to Titus, whom he refers to as a "true child," from God the Father and Christ Jesus our Lord. "True" can be translated as "genuine," being a term in Greek literature to describe children born in legitimate marriages. What is subtly implied is that Titus, in contrast to other professing leaders, is Paul's true representative. Much in the same way Paul has been entrusted to carry out the will of God and to communicate a message from Christ Jesus, so too Titus has been entrusted to carry out the apostle's directives and exhortations contained in the letter to progress the faith of the elect.

REFLECTIONS ON CHURCH

We have witnessed the abuse of authority in so many different realms that many of us have become altogether suspicious of authority. In particular, we have witnessed one scandal after another in religious institutions, where those who were entrusted as spiritual guides abused church finances and engaged in inappropriate relationships. It is easy to understand why many professing Christians prefer to simply attend worship services without becoming members: they do not want to subject themselves to church authority.

Paul himself was keenly aware of how spiritual authority could be abused. Later in this letter we will see how some would-be leaders used their authority for greedy gain. Nevertheless, the solution, according to the apostle, is not to disregard authority altogether but to recognize true authority. I am of the camp that believes the apostolic office is now closed and, as such, do not believe in contemporary apostles. Still, the Bible makes clear that we should submit to those who serve as elders and deacons in our churches, especially those in teaching capacities and who hold fast to the gospel. In a word, while authority will continue to be abused, the solution is not to disregard it altogether but to recognize those whom Paul would have considered true children because of their faithfulness to his gospel.

Along with the need to recover, recognize, and submit to true leadership is a renewed commitment to true faith. A word from the letter of James is fitting here: "You believe that God is one. Good! Even the demons believe—and shudder!" (2:19). James's point is that anyone—even demons—can have faith. But the kind of faith that characterizes God's chosen people and which is considered saving faith in the Bible is a faith that both embraces the truth concerning eternal life and recognizes the importance of godliness expressed in good works.

REFLECTIONS ON CULTURE

I used to believe that non-Christians were averse to the Christian faith because of its absolute claims (e.g., You have to believe in Jesus Christ to be saved). While this may still be the case, over the years I have noticed that non-Christians seem to have more of a problem with professing Christians than the content of orthodox Christianity itself. In a word, they are either turned off by the hypocrisy of believers or the apparent pointlessness of believing in Jesus given that Christianity seems to have little impact on the way Christians actually live.

I have had the privilege of working at some reputable companies and getting an MBA at the George Washington University School of Business. Throughout these experiences the thought occurred to me on more than one occasion that true believers would do very well in honest businesses that value integrity, diligence, and thoughtfulness. Christians, therefore, may want to consider whether non-Christians are turned off by them—not because of their commitment to their convictions but simply because they are distasteful in their character. What would happen if our faith was more authentic, i.e., if our faith exuded grace and humility in response to the gift of eternal life and was coupled with a commitment to respectable good works?

Perhaps more people would be drawn to at least consider the difference true faith makes. We are, after all, living in a time where people are yearning for something to believe in and for credible witnesses to that something.

DISCUSSION QUESTIONS

1. What attributes about God have you learned from this section in Titus?

2. How does being called by God and into Christ's service result in both humility and confidence? (Consider the example of Paul, the slave of God, apostle of Christ Jesus.)

3. Explain the two complementary components of true faith, i.e., "the faith of God's elect." Are these elements evident in your own profession of faith?

4. What is Christian hope? Why is Christian hope a sure hope—a hope that will not fail?

5. What is your attitude towards church authority? How do our reflections affect your view?

6. Do you think that non-Christians take issue more with the absolute claims of the Christian faith or the behavior of professing Christians?

3

Irreproachable Leaders

Titus 1:5–16 centers on the topic of irreproachable leaders and addresses it by way of contrast between ideal elders and false teachers. Therefore, the passage divides itself naturally into two parts:

1:5–9   The Irreproachable Elder

1:10–16   False Teachers

Paul begins this passage by focusing the audience on why he left Titus in Crete—"to appoint elders in every city." There is a word play in this verse, which should read something like, "I left you in Crete for this reason, that you might complete what was left undone" i.e., that you might appoint elders. The absence of an opening thanksgiving prayer that we find in some of Paul's other letters suggests that this task is especially urgent. That Titus has authority to establish authority—that he does not act according to his own accord—is highlighted by the somewhat superfluous way the verse ends—"As I [Paul] directed you."

In verses 6–9 Paul details the sort of man Titus is to appoint. Instead of detailing the meaning of each qualification (the standard commentaries on the Pastoral Epistles have already done this), I want to make several general comments. First, there is a priority placed on the candidate's domestic life: first and foremost, he must be a faithful husband and responsible father (1:6). What seems implicit is that a person who is unable to manage his own household is unqualified to manage a church, which is the household of God. Second, it is insufficient for the candidate to lack negative qualities; rather, he must also exhibit the qualities of hospitality, self-control, and righteousness (1:7–8). In other words, a candidate is not qualified simply because he is *not* a bad fellow; rather, he must also demonstrate positive qualities evident to all who know him. Finally, the candidate must hold fast to the Word—the word of God communicated through the apostle's proclamation (1:3), to carry out the related tasks of exhorting believers according to truth and reproving opponents of the faith (1:9). What is especially important to observe here is that a person is not necessarily qualified because he has enjoyed worldly success; rather, he becomes qualified as a result of being a disciple of the word of God. In summary, those who are faithful husbands and responsible fathers, who lack negative qualities and exhibit positive attributes, and who hold fast to the truth are model leaders for the churches in Crete.

In the next sub-unit, Paul explains why it is necessary for Titus to prioritize the appointment of elders: "For there are many rebels, empty-talkers, and deceivers, especially those from the Jewish group" (1:10). This description stands in stark contrast to both Paul and the elders. Paul submits himself as a slave to God his master; these rebels disregard authority. Paul has proclaimed the word of God, and elders are those who hold fast to Paul's teaching; these empty-talkers speak nonsense. Paul communicates truth as an apostle of Jesus Christ; these deceivers utter lies. Verse 12 suggests that these rebels, empty-talkers, and deceivers are from Crete, but have been influenced by Jewish teaching (1:14).

Unabashedly, Paul says that these troublemakers must be silenced because they are leading other believers astray by teaching what is inappropriate (1:11). He notes further that these teachers are "greedy for gain," in contrast to the model elder who "must not be greedy for gain" (1:6). Although Paul does not detail the content of their teaching, verse 11 suggests that these teachers are saying whatever appeals to people and results in financial gain (e.g., the health-and-wealth gospel). Thus, it becomes clear why the elder's work of exhortation and reproof is necessary. Elders must exhort the saints according to truth, given many have already begun to go astray. And elders must reprove these false teachers who are disrupting the peace of the churches and overturning many people's faith.

In the closing verses of the first chapter, Paul engages in a wholesale condemnation of these troublemakers. First, he borrows a quote from a Cretan prophet to highlight that these false teachers embody every stereotypical Cretan vice: "Cretans are always liars, evil beasts, and lazy gluttons" (1:12). After affirming this testimony, he reiterates the need to reprove those who waste time by paying attention to Jewish teaching instead of God's word (1:13–14). Finally, contrasting them with true believers whom Paul categorizes as "pure for whom all things are pure," he says that both their mind and conscience are tainted (1:15). That this is the case is manifested in their empty confession of God: "God they confess to know, but by their works they deny" (1:16a). Paul concludes his condemnation by stating that such false teachers are "vile and disobedient and unfit for any good work" (1:16b).

Indeed, these false teachers embody the antithesis of true faith. In the opening verse of the letter, Paul made clear that true faith must consist of an embrace of truth that is coupled with godliness. These false teachers, however, claim intimate knowledge of God but invalidate their confession by their shameful lives, specifically in their bad works. For this reason, they are unqualified for all good work, but especially the work of leading God's people. Only those who exhibit godliness within their homes and are known for their commendable lives and hold fast to the revealed truth are considered—like Titus, Paul's genuine child—true leaders by the apostle.

REFLECTIONS ON CHURCH

Churches would greatly benefit if they took seriously the teaching provided here concerning legitimate church leadership. I have witnessed too many churches select leaders on the basis of popularity and longevity in the church. Neither likability nor extensive presence automatically qualifies one to serve in the capacity of an elder. Rather, a potential elder must have a wife who is his number one advocate, who can say without reservation that the godly man at church is no less godly in his conduct toward his spouse and children. A potential elder must also have the respect of outsiders—his colleagues at work ought to say that he is above reproach. Finally, a potential elder must have a high view of the Word, expressed in a deep commitment to studying it and leading the saints accordingly. While churches often face different pressures to appoint elders in reaction to some circumstance (e.g., an elder is needed to help keep the senior pastor accountable), they must never sacrifice biblical guidance for the sake of expediency.

There is a quality that is implied in 1:5–9 and worthwhile to bring out and reflect on further. That is the quality of courage. It is one thing to be a diligent student of Scripture; it is another thing to be a speaker of truth. No one likes being told how to live, and few people welcome criticism and correction. But if the elder remains silent despite the obvious presence of sin or chooses to only say what people want to hear, then he is not substantially different from the empty-talkers who speak what is agreeable to people and thus lucrative. Therefore, the elder ought to remember that he ultimately stands before the Audience of One who has entrusted him to be a proclaimer of truth to the people of God. By doing so, the elder is able to find sufficient courage to engage in the difficult but necessary task of exhorting with sound doctrine and reproving troublemakers.

REFLECTIONS ON CULTURE

Rick Warren, author of the runaway bestseller *Purpose Driven Life*, is a Christian leader whom I have come to deeply respect. He is not only a prominent figure among Christians, but he has also gained the respect of non-Christians, having been invited to speak at prestigious universities and events on various topics including leadership, world hunger, and AIDS. He is one of the few Christian leaders who has proven that it is possible to be faithful to the gospel message and to gain a hearing among unbelievers. He illustrates that non-Christians will grant Christians a hearing when the latter demonstrate by their lifestyle that they indeed have a worthwhile message to consider.

I think there was a purpose in the sequence of qualifications listed by the apostle (without overstating the point). The last qualification pertains to speaking the truth of the gospel, but this quality is preceded by the requisites of being a devoted husband and father and having a good reputation among all people. The sequence of these qualifications may reflect Paul's understanding of the basic principle that a person must win credibility before he is able to speak effectively. Nowadays it is almost a given that church leaders—especially pastors—are no different from the average Joe. In fact, pastors—like politicians—have become notorious for infidelity, greed, and sloth. Like the false teachers who embodied the Cretan stereotype, pastors today seem to possess every typical vice. Pastors and churches alike must realize that to be more effective in their witness, they must adopt more rigorous standards for those who occupy leadership positions. As Paul exhorts in this passage, Christian leaders must strive to be above reproach if they are to gain a hearing.

DISCUSSION QUESTIONS

1. What attributes about God have you learned from this section in Titus?

2. Why does Paul prioritize the appointment of good leaders, specifically blameless elders? Do leadership development and selection have a high priority in your church? What happens to a church when it exists without such leaders?

3. Review the qualifications for elder candidates listed in 1:5–9. Discuss the meaning of the various qualifications and why you think they are necessary for elders to have.

4. What are some notable qualities of the troublemakers in Crete? What is *the* outstanding quality of these troublemakers? What are some contemporary parallels?

5. The church is, indeed, a place for sinners. Why is it important, nevertheless, to identify troublemakers? Describe an experience when troublemakers were left unchecked.

6. Why is courage an especially important quality for elders?

4

Theocentric Household[1]

REFLECTIONS ON TITUS 2:1-15

Titus 2:1-15 divides naturally into two related sections. The first half (2:1-10) focuses on the proper conduct expected of all who belong to the household of God. The second half (2:11-15) provides the basis for this conduct.[2] A simple outline, therefore, for the passage is:

2:1-10   The Godly Conduct Expected of the Various Members of God's Household

2:11-15   The Redemptive Basis for Godly Conduct

Rather than detailing the exhortations given to the various members of God's household—the older men (2:2), the older women (2:3), the younger women (2:4-5), the

1. The Greek word for God is *theos*. "Theocentric Household," therefore, expresses a household that centers on God.

2. In theological discourse, this dynamic is usually expressed as the indicative-imperative: we ought to live a particular way as followers of Jesus Christ (the imperative) in response to the grace that God has manifested in the work of redemption (the indicative).

younger men (2:6), Titus (2:7–8), and slaves (2:9–10)[3]—I want to make four general remarks regarding the first half of this chapter.

First, Titus is not instructed to teach sound doctrine *per se* in 2:1, but to teach the kind of lifestyle that accords with sound doctrine. Paul is not minimizing the importance of sound doctrine, for it provides the basis for advocating a particular lifestyle. Nevertheless, the focus of Paul's exhortation to Titus in the opening verse is to "teach what accords with sound doctrine." Plainly put, Titus is to instruct Cretan believers on the kind of lifestyle appropriate for those who profess to know God, in contrast to the troublemakers who invalidate their confession of faith by their evil deeds (1:16). In 2:1–10 Paul provides some suggestions as to what he has in mind for the various household members.

Second, believers are to view one another as family members as a result of their common faith in the way Paul views Titus as his true child because of their common faith. That Paul views churches as family households was already suggested in 1:7 where he compared the elder to a household manager. As members of God's household, believers are all interconnected and ought to take ownership for one another in the way parents take ownership of their own children and in the way siblings take ownership of one another. For this reason, Paul exhorts the older women to take an active role in training the younger women to be lovers of their husbands and children (2:4). Similarly, Titus and the older men are to present themselves as models of good works for the younger men, showing integrity in their teaching and conduct (2:7). In

3. See n. 2.

summary, believers are to understand their salvation not only in personal categories ("God saved me"), but also only in terms of community ("God has brought me into his family"). A personal commitment to God, then, entails a profound commitment to his family, which consists of the various members of his household.

Third, the quality that appears frequently in this passage relates to being temperate. The Greek adjective is *sōphōn* and indicates the ability to curb desires and impulses to produce a specific outcome. Athletes, for instance, usually exhibit a tremendous amount of temperance to succeed. This adjective and its cognates occur four times in these ten verses: older men are to be temperate (2:2); older women are to exhibit restraint so that they might train the younger women to be temperate (2:4); the younger women are also explicitly commanded to be temperate (2:5); the same is said to the younger men (2:6). In the second half of this chapter Paul will detail why all Christians ought to exhibit temperance. But the basic message is that living intentionally should be true of all believers in view of what God has done in Christ Jesus.

Finally, there are two refrains that we should observe. Verse 5 concludes on the note "*that* the word of God may not be reviled," and verse 10, "*that* they may adorn the doctrine of God our Savior." In other words, Paul's concern is not merely for good conduct in and of itself. Instead, he recognizes that believers' conduct will impact the reputation and reception of the word of God and the doctrine of God our Savior. The false teachers embody every stereotypical Cretan vice; therefore, the word of God is rejected as an effective means of personal transformation. If at the end of the day, adherence to the doctrine of God effects no positive transformation, then it is reviled and rejected. For this reason, the Cretan believers must be all the more intentional and careful that they are living according to sound doctrine so that the word of God would be exalted and the doctrine of God revered. In short, there is a missiological purpose for Christian conduct.

The second half of the chapter gives the basis for Christian conduct (notice the "for" in the beginning of 2:11). In the Greek, verses 11–14 make up a single sentence, interconnecting the past, future, and present. In the past, the grace of God has been manifested in Jesus Christ, bringing salvation to all types of people—from every tribe, tongue, and nation and from every socio-economic group (2:11). In the future, this same Jesus will appear, and during this time those who have awaited his return will share in his glory (2:13). In the present, all believers are to live intentionally, on the one hand rejecting ungodliness and worldly passions, on the other hand pursuing temperance, righteousness, and godliness (2:12). In summary, believers have a distinct way of looking at both the past and future, which, in turn, should influence the way they live in the present.

Verse 14 goes into some detail about Christ's self-sacrifice. Paul highlights how Christ gave himself up to redeem believers from all lawlessness and to purify for himself a people who are zealous for good works. Paul does not suggest that Christ has freed believers so that they are now free to live however they please. Rather, it is more appropriate to think of redemption in terms of transference from one kingdom to another. Previously, believers were under the power of sin and thus lived according to lawlessness. Now, however, having been cleansed by the blood of Christ they belong to a new kingdom and thus ought to pursue lifestyles that reflect their new allegiance.

The apostle concludes chapter two by reiterating the command to Titus to teach, exhort, and reprove with all authority. He reminds Titus that he has authority because he has been commissioned by the apostle. Therefore, despite whatever opposition he may face in instructing the various members of God's household on proper conduct, he is not to let anyone disregard him. In view of the first and second appearance of Christ Jesus, all believers are to live in a manner that shows they belong to God's family and that brings honor to the word of God. To accomplish this, Titus and future elders must engage in the work of exhorting and reproving God's people according to sound doctrine.

REFLECTIONS ON CHURCH

The application of this second chapter to churches today is obvious enough that little comment is needed. Therefore, I will confine this section to two reflections.

First, given the spread of the Internet, some professing believers are inclined to simply download sermons from popular preachers on Sundays and consider that their act of worship. They suppose that so long as their personal relationship with God seems vibrant, all is well. This chapter, however, reminds us of the importance of connecting with the people of God. To be sure, churches can be ugly places (which is to be expected, given they were always intended to be a place for sinners), and so the temptation to isolate oneself from church and to focus on one's individual relationship with God and perhaps with a select group of Christians is certainly understandable. But an unavoidable aspect of the gospel is that not only has God saved us but he has also brought us into his family. Therefore, it is impossible to claim allegiance to Christ, who is the head of the church, and yet disregard the Church, which is his body. A truly vibrant faith, then, must include a serious commitment to live in community with all types of believers who belong to the household of God.

Second, a clear dynamic is at work in this chapter. In summary, Christians ought to live a particular way in view of what they believe. Far too many believers have a shallow faith that supposes that so long as one believes in God, all will be well. While it is true that we are saved by faith alone, saving faith never exists in isolation. Rather, saving faith is always accompanied by a distinct lifestyle so that the absence of a zeal for good works suggests the absence of true saving faith. If, indeed, we believe that Christ appeared to redeem us from the power of sin and that someday he will appear again in full glory to consummate the work that he has already begun, then our lives should be characterized by a constant rejection of worldly passions and the pursuit of righteousness. In short, the gospel should create very intentional people who focus their lives on doing good works—not to be saved, but because they know that they have already been saved and will enter into glory with Christ's return. Any faith devoid of such intentionality is not the kind of faith that belongs to God's chosen people

REFLECTIONS ON CULTURE

Twice in this chapter Paul highlights the relationship between Christian conduct and the reputation and reception of the gospel. In 2:5 he exhorts the younger women to be self-controlled, pure, and good wives and mothers so that the word of God may not be reviled. In 2:10 he exhorts slaves to be trustworthy so that their masters may adorn the doctrine of God our Savior. The clear implication is that when professing believers act like the Cretans, being dishonest, evil, and lazy, then those outside of the faith simply cannot take the word of God seriously. If at the end of the day it appears that the doctrine of God revealed in Paul's gospel effects little change, then the obvious question is, "Why bother with something that, at best, makes no difference on my life, and at worst, makes me a hypocrite?"

In the next chapter, the apostle addresses more directly the question of how believers ought to engage society, specifically those outside of the church. But his specific concern in chapter two is their relationship with one another as members of God's household and how the world will respond. The way believers care for one another and exhort and reprove one another to live commendably will, in the eyes of the apostle, cause the watching world to respect and adorn the word of God or to revile and despise it. Again, one must wonder how much of the hostility towards Christianity today is a result of the truths it espouses or a result of the conduct of its followers, especially in the way they relate to one another.

DISCUSSION QUESTIONS

1. What attributes about God have you learned from this section in Titus?

2. Do you view your church as God's household and the church members as family members? How would your faith change if you saw the church and church members as such?

3. What are some areas where God is calling you to be more temperate in light of the Christian confession that Christ has come and will come again?

4. What is the problem with doing church in isolation—listening to sermons on the radio, television, or Internet instead of becoming a vibrant member of a local church?

5. Would your friends and family describe you as a deliberate person? Why is being intentional a basic Christian quality?

6. How is your daily conduct helping or hurting the reputation and reception of the word of God?

5

Upright Citizens

L IKE THE previous section, Titus 3:1–7 divides naturally into two related sections. The first half (3:1–2) focuses on how believers should behave as upright citizens, especially towards those in authority. The second half (3:3–8a) provides the basis for why they should be model citizens. Again, the indicative-imperative dynamic is at work: in view of what God has done, this is how they ought to live. A simple outline for the passage is:

3:1–2   Godly Conduct to Those Outside of the Church

3:3–8a The Redemptive Basis for Such Godly Conduct

It appears that the Cretan believers have forgotten some basic instruction they had received concerning their calling to live as upright citizens, especially with respect to those in authority. Therefore, Paul begins this chapter by reminding them "to be submissive to ruling authorities" (i.e., to be obedient and ready for every good work). What is notable here is that a clear contrast is implied with the troublemakers whom Paul refers to as rebels who are unfit for every good work (1:10–16). In effect Paul is exhorting his audience not to be like the false teachers. Paul then expands his instruction on being upright citizens by commanding the Cretan believers to slander none, to be peaceable and gentle, and to show meekness to all people (3:2), not simply to those in authority.

The second half of this section is rich with meaning. This is in part because it is one of the few explicit summaries in the New Testament of how the different persons of the Trinity (God the Father, God the Son, and God the Holy Spirit) work together to accomplish salvation. Paul begins this section by inviting the Cretan believers to recall that they too—Paul, Titus, and the audience members—were once no different from those outside of the faith: "For we *ourselves* were once foolish, disobedient, deluded, enslaved to all kinds of passions and pleasures, living in malice and envy, hated and hating one another" (3:3). In other words, Paul is saying that *previously* it was perfectly natural—it was to be expected—that they too would be rebellious against those in authority, disobedient, unfit for every good work, slanderers, quarrelers, harsh, and overbearing because they too were once walking the downward spiral of mutual hatred.

The next four verses make up a single sentence in the Greek. The sentence—if translated woodenly—is awkward because Paul is trying to pack multiple related ideas together. First, echoing 2:11, Paul refers to the appearance of God's goodness and loving-kindness in the person of Jesus Christ (3:4). He then interrupts his train of thought to highlight that believers have been saved not because of their righteous works but because of God's mercy (3:5a); therefore, believers should not look at their salvation as grounds for boasting. Paul then describes how believers have been cleansed through the renewing work of the Holy Spirit, whom God the Father has poured out richly through Christ Jesus, His Son and our Savior (3:5b-6). Having been declared righteous by his grace, believers have become heirs according to God's great plan to bestow eternal life on his chosen ones (3:7).

Verse 3:8 is a fitting conclusion to this section. Paul accentuates how this "saying"—the confession summarized in 3:3-7—"is trustworthy." Thus, Titus is not to deviate from it like the false teachers but to insist upon it, so that "those who have believed in God may be careful to devote themselves to good works." In summary, all believers once lived in foolishness, disobedience, deceit, and hatred; thus, being rebellious, slanderous, and pompous was to be expected—indeed, they were unfit for any kind of commendable work. But now, having experienced the grace of God that saved them not as a result of their righteous works but God's mercy, they have been made new and now possess the power of the Holy Spirit to do what they could not do before—to devote themselves to good works.

REFLECTIONS ON CHURCH

Gospel-living is still grossly misunderstood today. There is still the age-old problem that some believe God saves according to righteous deeds. Thus, the gospel boils down to the ditty, "You better watch out, you better not cry, you better be good I'm telling you why—Jesus is coming to town." In other words, we relate to God as if He simply rewards good behavior and punishes bad. As a result, any good deed done on our part is for the sake of being accepted.

Others suppose that gospel-living is believing in your best life now—as if God were some sort of genie who existed to realize every one of our earthly desires. The health-and-wealth gospel is still very much in vogue with a number of mega-churches still holding to the belief that our biggest problem is that although God wants to bless us with one material blessing after another, we dream too small. Faith, then, is believing that God will grant all our dreams—and more if we just believe.

The saying that is trustworthy and which needs to be reiterated among churches today is nicely summarized for us in Titus 3:3–7. Believers should never feel superior to anyone else on account of their salvation, for we too once lived in darkness, lying to and hating one another and being enslaved to all kinds of passions. But the gospel says that God revealed his kindness to us through his Son—not because we accomplished anything good on our end to merit his goodness but purely on account of his grace. Moreover, we have not only been renewed and empowered by the Spirit to live a life devoted to good works, but we have now been made righteous and look forward to receiving eternal life when Christ returns. This is the gospel, and this is the only basis and purpose for good works. We do not pursue good works to be saved; we do so because we are already saved. We do not pursue our best life now because we await the blessed eternal life that will be ours on the Day of the Lord. In the meantime, now that we are a new creation in

Christ and have received the empowering presence of the Holy Spirit, we are to devote ourselves to good works. The gospel, then, needs to be guarded and reiterated so that God's people may rightly understand the place and importance of good works.

REFLECTIONS ON CULTURE

Throughout this book I have reiterated the important role good works play in our proclamation of the gospel. If there is nothing attractive about our behavior, then there is little reason for those outside of the faith to even consider the gospel message. But imagine walking down the street and passing by a bakery. You are almost enchanted by the smell and cannot help but follow the aroma into the bakery. Then you begin to look at the freshly baked treats and even allow yourself to listen to the salesperson describe how everything was prepared just a few hours ago with the finest ingredients to justify the exorbitant prices.

The gospel itself is offensive because we are a resume-driven culture, i.e., we like to believe that everything we possess is a result of our own effort. Therefore, a gospel that declares that we are saved not by our works but by God's mercy is inherently difficult to believe. There is no reason, then, to add another obstacle by being unduly offensive. Instead, if Christians became model citizens, respecting all those in authority; if they stopped joining their colleagues in ridiculing their boss; if they were peaceable, gentle, and respectful to all instead of having to win every argument and have the last word; if they exuded humility out of recognition that they were no better than those commonly tagged as sinners; one can only imagine how unbelievers would find something attractive about the faith. The apostle was not naïve in supposing that all would come to believe if believers just got their act together. But he did hope that even those who rejected the faith would respect the faith because of its representatives and that perhaps even some would be won as a result of the way Christians conduct themselves as upright citizens.

DISCUSSION QUESTIONS

1. What attributes about God have you learned from this section in Titus?

2. Summarize the organization of Titus 3:1–8a. How does it compare to Titus 2:1–15? What does the arrangement teach about the dynamic of the Christian life?

3. How would you apply the instructions Paul gives in 3:1–2 on being upright and commendable citizens? What areas are lacking in your life and in need of improvement?

4. How does the gospel invite us to view those who speak maliciously of others, who are belligerent and overbearing (3:3)?

5. According to what basis did God save us? What impact should this truth have on our lives?

6. How does the gospel create a people who are careful to devote themselves to good works?

7. How is gospel-living misunderstood today? What impact do these misunderstandings have on the way Christians live?

6

Steadfast Devotion to Good Works

REFLECTIONS ON TITUS 3:8B–15

THE LAST section consists of a series of instructions, which wrap up key themes in the letter. It can be broken down to four parts:

3:8b–9   What Is Useful versus Useless

3:10–11   Concerning the Divisive Person

3:12–14   Some Personal Instructions

3:15   Final Greetings

Earlier in the letter Paul noted how false teachers were upsetting the faith of whole families by teaching what they should not for shameful gain (1:11). As a result of paying attention to such false teaching, the Cretan believers were behaving improperly, both with respect to one another (2:1–10) and towards those outside of the faith (3:1–2). For this reason, Paul exhorts Titus to repeatedly set before them sound doctrine and the appropriate lifestyle that should follow, for only "such things are excellent and useful for people" (3:8b). In contrast, the teachings of the troublemakers, which consist of "foolish controversies, genealogies, debates, and quarrels about the law, are useless and worthless" (3:9). Consequently, Paul commands Titus and the Cretan believers to "avoid" them and to focus their attention and energy on preserving sound doctrine and devoting themselves to good works.

Although Paul devoted the past two sections on exhortations and reproofs to believers, he has not lost sight of the troublemakers who have made the appointment of sound elders so urgent. In 3:10–11 Paul again addresses the "person who stirs up division" and very plainly commands the community to break fellowship with such a fractious person after giving him several warnings (3:10). Then, echoing his harsh condemnation in 1:10–16, he dismisses such a person as being "warped, sinful, and willful" (3:11). Paul's concern here is not for the ignorant sinner but for the sinner who has been informed and warned and yet is determined to persist in sin. Paul aptly describes such a person as being "warped."

Paul's opening instructions to appoint elders suggested that Titus's stay in Crete was temporary—that Titus was dispatched for specific purposes and would soon rejoin the apostle. This is now made explicit in 3:12: "When I sent Artemas or Tychicus to you, make every effort to come to me at Nicopolis, for I have decided to winter there." Artemas or Tychicus is presumably Titus's replacement. The word in Greek for "to decide" is similar in form to the adjective "willful" in 3:11. Paul is communicating that he is just as determined to stay in Nicopolis as the willful sinner is resolved to cause division. This was no small thing, given

Nicopolis was known for its harsh winters. By communicating his decision to stay the winter in a severe region, Paul contrasts himself again with the troublemakers who are gluttonous, lazy, and greedy for gain. The recipients of this letter, therefore, understand a stark contrast is being presented to them and are inspired to follow Paul's example of suffering for the gospel instead of using it as a means for personal gain.

Paul also instructs Titus to send Zenas and Apollos on their way and to make sure all their needs are adequately provided for by the Cretan believers (3:13). The mention of Zenas and Apollos is certainly not random. Just a few verses before, Paul highlighted how those who have believed in God ought to be careful to devote themselves to good works (3:8). This general principle is repeated in 3:14 but applied more specifically: "And let our people learn to devote themselves to good works, to meet urgent needs so that they might not be unfruitful." The obvious good work Paul has in mind is meeting the immediate needs of Zenas and Apollos. In addition, Paul's language "let *our* people" reiterates the difference between those who exhibit true faith like Paul and Titus by devoting themselves to good works and those who profess to know God but deny him by their deplorable deeds (1:16). As a fitting conclusion to the letter, Paul highlights how true faith—the faith of God's elect—must always be accompanied by a tangible commitment to live commendably in the form of good works.

The letter concludes with a series of greetings (3:15). First, Paul notes that all who are with him send greetings. Then he instructs Titus to greet specifically "those who love us in the faith." This specification serves almost as a challenge to the recipients of this letter, which includes more than Titus as the final blessing, "Grace be with *you all*," indicates. Throughout the letter the audience members have experienced a comparison. Paul is a slave of God and apostle of Christ Jesus who has been uniquely entrusted to proclaim the word of God concerning eternal life. He has been faithfully carrying out this work as Christ's representative by writing this letter, which reiterates the fundamentals of his gospel and the steadfast devotion to good works that should accompany true faith. Titus also is Paul's true child in the faith, progressing the work begun by the apostle by appointing elders and exhorting and reproving the Cretan believers to proper conduct, both within God's household and towards those outside the faith. He models the behavior and work that the future elders will continue. In stark contrast, the troublemakers who are characterized by insubordination, deceit, and greed profess to know God—they claim to have a deeply personal relationship with God—but deny him by the way they live and prove that they are unfit for any good work. Some among the Cretan believers have already begun to subscribe to their teaching and way of life. Paul, therefore, concludes this letter by implicitly challenging the audience members to consider whether they love "us"—the apostle and Titus—and, thus, share in a common faith, or the troublemakers who lack true faith. Paul concludes the letter by praying that God would grant all of them grace to make the right decision and to maintain a steadfast devotion to good works in accordance with true faith.

REFLECTIONS ON CHURCH

Admittedly, Titus closes on a somewhat harsh note. We will observe and reflect on just two points.

First, Paul knows how easy it is for people to agree that true believers should devote themselves to good works. It would be very difficult to find a professing Christian that does not believe this. But—as the apostle has highlighted throughout this letter—it is not enough to simply agree with the principle; one must also put it into practice. For this reason, he exhorted the Cretan believers to meet the immediate needs of Zenas and Apollos. Similarly, he would exhort those of us today who agree with the principle of good works but suppose that we will seriously engage in them sometime in the future when we have more time and money to start practicing good works. In addition, to those who claim that they want to help people but do not know how to, the apostle would remind them that there is no shortage of needs and that such needs would become evident if we looked just a little more carefully at those around us. To be sure, people are generally hesitant to express their need for help, but it does not take a genius to recognize that a single mother with three children is hurting for help; or that a woman struggling with infertility while her friends celebrate the birth of another child would benefit from some compassion; or that perhaps one should support a child from World Vision instead of purchasing another television because bigger is supposedly better. The apostle is inviting us to be honest with ourselves. Do you agree that those who believe in God should devote themselves to good works? If so, Paul exhorts us to simply look around and to see what we can do here and now to meet immediate needs by sharing our time and resources instead of simply agreeing to the principle of devoting oneself to good works.

Second, Paul challenges us to be thoughtful about the road we are "traveling." There are very few people—if any—that walk a road that has not already been taken. For this reason the apostle consistently challenged the Cretan believers to consider the question of which road they are traveling—that of Paul and Titus or that of the false teachers. Similarly, the challenge is put to us today to think about who our real teachers and mentors are. Although we may claim allegiance to Christ or the apostle or our Sunday school teacher, in reality we may be following the path of the greedy businessman who lives only for himself. Perhaps we are scared to think in these terms, lest we give the impression of being exclusive and divisive. But I think our culture is beyond the point of supposing that all roads are the same and lead to the same outcome. And so Paul's concluding challenge is worthwhile to consider, both individually and corporately: Whom/what do you really love? What dream are you really pursuing? Who is your real master?

REFLECTIONS ON CULTURE

It is somewhat refreshing that many seeker-friendly churches have now openly admitted that their approach to evangelism is ineffective in the long-run. All churches and denominations are full of problems and have made their share of mistakes, but it is refreshing for a group to be honest about it so that others would learn from their mistakes.

Broadly put, what these churches came to realize was that in their attempt to be seeker-friendly, i.e., to adjust their programs, worship, and even the content of their teaching to be agreeable to secular culture, they lost their unique identity in Christ and forgot their calling to be holy (set apart). What they have come to recognize is that those who are spiritually curious or hunger are not looking for churches that reflect contemporary musical concerts but transcendence. In a word, they are looking for a community that teaches and lives differently from anything else that can be found in mainstream culture.

Many believers today are still hesitant about preserving sound doctrine lest they be categorized as dogmatic. Many churches are afraid to practice church discipline lest they be dismissed as exclusive and discriminatory. Many church leaders are afraid to exhort and reprove in specific ways lest they experience a decline in church attendance. But the reality is that we will never be able to offer anything different—anything truly transcendent and beautiful—unless we have the courage to discern what is true and useful, to practice church discipline, and to speak gently and firmly about the nature of true faith, expressed in a steadfast devotion to good works.

DISCUSSION QUESTIONS

1. What attributes about God have you learned from this section in Titus?

2. Proverbs 23:7 says, "As a man thinks in his heart, so is he." How is the principle illustrated in this letter (see

3:8b-9)? What does your mind tend to dwell on? How does this impact the way you live?

3. Paul instructs the Cretan believers to break fellowship with the willful sinner. Describe a situation in your church experience when a fractious person was left unchecked. What impact did it have on the individual? On the community?

4. Do you have people like the apostle Paul in your life who exemplifies what it means to suffer for the gospel? Why it is so important to have such models of true faith?

5. What are some present and immediate ways you can help meet the needs of those who have less?

6. Why is it so important for churches to care about sound doctrine, to practice church discipline, and to create a culture where it is normal to exhort and reprove one another in specific ways? How do these relate to their ability to minister as salt and light of the world?

7

Conclusion

IN THE preceding chapters we have briefly considered the message and flow of Paul's letter to Titus using the name TITUS itself as acronym to cover the major themes: T—True Faith (1:1–4); I—Irreproachable Elders (1:5–16); T—Theocentric Household (2:1–15); U—Upright Citizens (3:1–8a); and S—Steadfast Devotion to Good Works (3:8b–16). Here we will summarize our reflections and consider how they are interwoven.

In the first section, Paul communicates that he is a slave of God and apostle of Christ Jesus who has been commissioned to advance the faith of God's elect. Specifically, he has been called to further their embrace of the truth, which must be accompanied by godliness and expressed in the form of commendable living. Such is the nature of true faith. He highlights his unique role in history as the one who has been entrusted with the word of God concerning eternal life, which was promised before the world was formed but has now been revealed through the apostle's proclamation. For this reason, he is to be recognized as one with authority and his gospel as the only source for true faith.

In the second section, Paul urges Titus to begin the work of appointing irreproachable elders. Such prospective leaders must be faithful husbands, devoted fathers, known for their hospitality, commitment to good works, and temperance, and must be devoted to studying the word of God and exhorting and reproving accordingly. This extensive list details what Paul means by being a steward of God who is above reproach.

This particular task is especially urgent because there are troublemakers who are upsetting the faith of many believers. They embody every typical Cretan vice, being rebellious, dishonest, greedy, gluttonous, and lazy. But most notably they lack true faith, for although they profess to know God, they deny him by their works; i.e., they do not live commendably and, therefore, prove that they do not have the kind of faith expected of those who belong to God's chosen people. As such they are not only unfit for every good work, but also are unqualified to serve as church leaders. The audience members, then, are to look only to Titus and to elders who meet the high calling to be above reproach for true leadership.

The third section focuses on how the various members of God's household should conduct themselves, especially with respect to one another. Paul's basic framework is that all believers ought to view one another as family members because they share a common faith and should, therefore, care for one another accordingly. In addition, all of them are called to live temperately so that their individual conduct and mutual devotion would bring honor to the word of God. In short, they are to be mindful that their lifestyles as members of God's household directly impact on how those outside of the faith will view the doctrine of God our savior.

In the second half of chapter two, Paul reminds the Cretan believers of the theological basis for their conduct. In this way, Paul reiterates the indicative-imperative dynamic of the Christian life—that what God has first done in showing mercy in Christ should shape the way we live. Specifically, Paul reminds the audience members that they have a worldview with a distinct way of looking at the past and future which, in turn, should govern the way they live in the present. Formerly, God revealed his grace by sending his Son, who has brought salvation to all types of people. In the future, the Son will come again in full glory to give eternal life to all those who have trusted in him and have awaited his return. In the present, then, believers are to renounce ungodliness and worldly passions and to pursue godliness and be zealous for good works. In the face of false teaching, Titus is not to shy from declaring these truths and exhorting and reproving with all authority.

In the fourth section, Paul reminds the audience how they are to conduct themselves towards those outside of the faith, especially to those in authority. They are to be respectful and upright citizens who lead the way in good works. In addition, they are to be kind to all people—not just to fellow believers and those in authority—by speaking ill of none, seeking peace, and exhibiting humility.

Similar to the third section, Paul explains the gospel-basis for these exhortations. Paul says that a rebellious attitude, disobedience, rudeness, and the like made sense before believers were transformed by the grace of God. He acknowledges that all believers were previously enslaved to foolishness, deceit, worldly passions, and mutual hatred. But now they are new people as a result of the Trinity—God the Father has poured out God the Spirit through God the Son, and thus we have been renewed and empowered to do what we could not on our own. Moreover, now that we have been made righteous, we have become co-heirs of glory according to God's wondrous plan to give eternal life to those who trust in Jesus Christ. *Because* believers have this confession and hope of eternal life—*in response* to what God has done—they are to be careful to devote themselves to good works. Again Paul highlights the integral role that Titus and the future elders play in insisting upon these doctrines and the nature of true faith given the presence and influence of the false teachers.

In the last section Paul provides a series of instructions, that loosely gravitate around the theme of being steadfast in one's devotion to good works. He begins by reiterating what is worthwhile for Titus to reiterate in his teaching in contrast to the troublemakers who are teaching what they should not for greedy gain. He then details how the believers should handle a divisive person. Finally, he provides specific instructions concerning several individuals, highlighting how the Cretan believers should meet the needs of Zenas and Apollos, and then concludes the letter with several greetings and a benediction. The letter concludes with an implicit challenge for its recipients to consider whether their allegiance is to Paul and Titus who exhibit true faith or to the false teachers who deny the sincerity of their faith through their misdeeds.

Despite its brevity, the letter to Titus is powerful and relevant today. In an age where Christianity is still the dominant world religion, it is a reminder of what the nature of true faith is. Also, it points to an obvious and increasing need to fill the leadership gap with qualified individuals who have demonstrated that they are above reproach. In addition, given the popular emphasis on one's individual relationship with God, the letter reminds us that we have not only been saved as individuals, but that we have also been brought into God's household and, therefore, must live out our faith in the context of gospel-community. Moreover, we are reminded that churches are not called to retreat from mainstream culture, but to engage it by living as upright and model citizens who are respectful of all and spearhead various efforts to bring about socio-economic good. Finally, the letter is a sobering reminder that believers are to adopt a steadfast devotion to good works. What this means is that now and always, as people who have been redeemed from all lawlessness and hope for eternal life, we are to pursue good works in every season of life, whether we are single and just beginning our careers, busy paying for our first home and being new parents, or retiring from work. Such is the nature and demands of true faith.

For Further Study

FOR A good introduction to Paul, I recommend Michael F. Bird, *Introducing Paul: The Man, His Mission, and His Message* (Downers Grove: InterVarsity, 2008). This book is a brief but comprehensive introduction to Paul's life and teaching.

There are not many commentaries written on just Titus. Instead, Titus tends to be discussed under the more general topic of the Pastoral Epistles, which includes 1 and 2 Timothy. Among these I recommend Ben Witherington III, *Letters and Homilies for Hellenized Christians: A Socio-Rhetorical Commentary on Titus, 1–2 Timothy, and 1–3 John* (Downers Grove: InterVarsity, 2007), a thick but worthwhile reference full of fresh insights and theological reflection. An excellent commentary, but difficult to access for those without a background in Greek, is Philip H. Towner's *The Letters to Timothy and Titus* (Grand Rapids: Eerdmans, 2006). Perhaps the reader may find more manageable, John Stott, *Guard the Truth: The Message of 1 Timothy and Titus* (Downers Grove: InterVarsity, 1996). Stott is always reliable. Finally, for a recent treatment on the theology of the Pastoral Epistles see Andreas J. Köstenberger (ed.), *Entrusted with the Gospel: Paul's Theology in the Pastoral Epistles* (Nashville: B&H Publishing Group, 2010).